shack chic

INNOVATION IN THE SHACK-LANDS OF SOUTH AFRICA

PHOTOGRAPHS BY CRAIG FRASER

Thames & Hudson

First published in the United Kingdom in 2002 by Thames & Hudson Ltd, 181A High Holborn, London WC1V 7QX

British Library Cataloguing-in-Publication Data
A catalogue record for this book is available from the British Library

ISBN 0-500-511055

Printed in Singapore

This book is dedicated to all shack dwellers
and their families,
especially those who welcomed us
into their homes.

We honour them and their achievements.

Enkosi.

'victory:
to build
a shack
and call it
home'

Sandile Dikeni

According to the South African National Population Census 96, the official terminology for shacks is 'informal housing settlement'. Indigenous words describing these structures include 'mkhukhu' (Zulu), 'blikhuis' or 'hokkie' (Afrikaans) and 'ityotyombe' (Xhosa). Besides these, however, there is a proliferation of other less complimentary terms that indicate that these dwellings do not always arouse positive interest or inspire a positive response.

Indeed, on the surface, these buildings do not boast any discernible architectural value. No wonder then that many count them to be of no particular social consequence. Added to this, their occupants are often resented and denounced as 'squatters' and land-grabbers.

So why call this book Shack Chic? Surely this is a contradiction in terms? Surely the two concepts must be mutually exclusive?

The word 'chic' conjures up manifestations of sophistication, elegance and style, beauty and refinement. In other words, deliberate and desirable aesthetic configurations.

On the other hand, when the word 'shack' comes to mind, the associations that quickly follow it are along the lines of 'temporary', 'impermanent', 'disorderly', 'illegal', 'unplanned', 'over-populated', 'dirty', 'depressing' and so on. Indeed, many shacks in informal housing settlements in South Africa are all these things.

The space between these two concepts is so wide in our perceptions that to suggest that they could possibly occur simultaneously is an almost shocking proposition.

The photographs contained in this book are a rebuttal against that thesis. They are a visual account of daily life as it is created and experienced by many of the 1,5 million shack-dwellers in South Africa.

This book is a documentary on the lives of 'previously disadvantaged' but presently determined, 'previously oppressed' but presently overcoming individuals.

It is about the dignity to be found in the dusty streets of South Africa's shack-lands. While these people obviously don't take pleasure in the poverty they live in, they stand proud in the face of it. These are people who are doing the best they can with the little they have and, in the process, coming up with something aesthetically unique and fresh to offer the world.

This is creativity and ingenuity.

This is Shack Chic.

'living
is worthless
for one without
a
home'

Ethiopian Proverb

setting a context

Well-known large informal housing settlements in Cape Town include Crossroads, Marconi Beam, Barcelona, KTC, Phola Park/ Waterfront, Sweet Home, Tambo Square, Boys Town, Brown's Farm, Joe Slovo Park, New Rest, Vietnam, Lwandle, Oostenberg, Happy Valley, Spandau, Bermuda, Victoria Myenge and Trevor Vilakazi.

In the main, these areas are populated by low-income earners and unemployed people. Among the few economically active residents, typical occupations include domestic help and manual labour such as gardening, painting and construction odd jobs. The average wage for a domestic helper or a labourer is ± R60/day and the average wage for a painter is ± R80-R120/day. On these kinds of budgets, and with the settlements showing 10% per annum compound growth, meeting basic human needs such as reliable energy/fuel, shelter, running water, refuse management and efficient sewerage systems is next to impossible.

Based on these measures, services, or lack thereof, in the informal settlements are the clearest indicators of social inequity, an apartheid hangover it will take years to recover from. Policing is inadequate and there is little or no access to public telephones, public transport, public hospitals and public schools. Air pollution from domestic fuels such as coal, wood and paraffin and industrial emissions from factories and mines is rife. And despite having so little in monetary value, the residents of these areas are not exempt from burglary and other crimes.

In such an environment, people's futures seem compromised literally from birth. Could anything positive come from such a negative beginning?

The evolutionary timeline of informal settlements goes back to the early 1900s during the gold rush when satellite migrant labour camps formed the earliest incarnation. People from the rural areas seeking work in urban centres, particularly in the area now known as Gauteng (in and around Johannesburg), made these designated areas of forced segregation their first port of call.

By 1950, there were 20 informal settlements in the country. In the Western Cape, the lure of the city was the promise of work in the burgeoning manufacturing industry, on the wine farms and in the fishing industry.

And, although there were many attempts to suppress the development of these areas (to contain the cholera outbreaks that were rife at this time as well as to enforce the Group Areas Act) by forcibly removing the residents, many of them grew and were formalised into what are now commonly known as townships.

However, by 1960, the population had doubled while the number of council properties remained static. With no rates being collected and no commercial or industrial activity to speak of anywhere within their vicinity, penury and destitution were the inevitable outcomes.

With the government easing up on the Group Areas Act in the mid-eighties, the dam walls began to crack. The townships began to develop organically and be populated by people who couldn't be absorbed into the national economic system (in the shape and form of the gold and diamond mines).

By 1994 the walls burst completely when the townships were inundated by a heavy influx of humanity from the rural areas, some simply hoping for a better future in the cities, while others were families coming to join the breadwinner in the 'city'.

Crossroads, Marconi Beam,
Barcelona, KTC,
Phola Park/Waterfront,
sweet
home
Tambo Square, Boys Town,
Brown's Farm, Joe Slovo Park,
New Rest,
Vietnam, Lwandle, Oostenberg,
Happy Valley,
Spandau, Bermuda,
Victoria Myenge
Trevor Vilakazi

'the more you move people around, the more you reinforce the stigma of exclusion'

Prof. John Abbott, University of Cape Town

This statement is so true of the informal settlements in the Western Cape. Rebuilding these neighbourhoods would help rebuild people's self-esteem. Although areas such as Crossroads are now well into their second and third generations, the memory of historical forced removals discourages many people from investing the time, effort or financial resources in their homes. There is a pervading sense of transience that discourages people from upgrading their properties structurally. As they live on the physical fringes of the cities, so they barely feature on the social, economic or political landscape.

Practical solutions are being sought to manage this untenable situation. Providing subsidised formal housing is one option to halt the growth of these rapidly growing zones of social and economic exclusion. However, the feasibility of such a program when the number of people to be resettled is 1,5 million, at a density of 200-500 people/ha, is questionable. Especially when one considers that the trend of in-migration and natural growth continues unchecked.

In the current world economy, personal value is often evaluated on the basis of economic status. So, when you live in a shack, what is your concept of home? What does it mean to own one? Can one actually be proud of the shack one lives in?

"After Murray and Roberts evicted us from its Ilangeni hostels in Guguletu, for participating in a strike, I went to stay at NY 21 NO20 in Guguletu, at Priest Ntlontla's house. After my wife left Transkei to live with me here I could not afford to pay rent at the Priest's house and I then moved to this place, in 1987.

At this time this place was called Brown's Farm, because we forcibly erected our shacks on Mr Brown's farm. We were always intimidated with forced removal but we won the battle, after which we renamed it, and it is now popularly known as Philippi. The first leader of Philippi was Toyise, who asked us to pay R250 for rent. During this period there was no water here, but after a protracted struggle and lobbying, which was led by him, as he was connected to the progressive movements at the time, a single tap was eventually installed and the entire camp was dependent on it."

THEMBA MAJEBE, A31, BROWN'S FARM, PHILIPPI

property
OWNership

Reflecting the historically low degree of security in tenure, as well as the abiding hope and expectation that in the new political dispensation there may exist opportunities to move into better areas, many shack owners (who tend to be the builders as well) are reluctant to invest substantially to convert an informal dwelling into something more permanent. This often results in people living in structurally compromised buildings for years.

Unlike similar settlements in other developing countries in Africa (which feature indigenous architecture in the form of mud / wattle huts or even stick / branch houses even in metropolitan contexts), the South African equivalents are constructed using leftover or recycled 'modern' materials such as wooden planks, chipboard, corrugated iron sheets, plastic sheeting, industrial tarpaulin, advertising boards, canvas and cardboard.

'hoUSeS are built on foundations with walls and roof. hOmes are built with things much deeper and less concrete'

Sandile Dikeni

architecture

'It's very important that even though a building may only be for temporary use,
it has to be pleasing to the eye – something of beauty.
A person has to be able to feel that this is home.'

SHIGERU BAN. JAPANESE ARCHITECT

The nature and sources of these building materials carry inherent limitations. As a result, structural deficiencies or architectural 'flaws' are inevitable.

But there is a system, believe it or not. One does not just arrive with a barrow-load of planks and start erecting a shack in any area. In the Western Cape, for instance, to be allowed to move into a particular neighbourhood, it is necessary to approach the community leaders in your prospective neighbourhood with a letter from the street committee in your previous area of residence vouching for your character. Criminal records and quarrelsome behaviour, for example, will diminish one's chances significantly.

No statistics could reveal the full truth of life as much as people themselves through the way they mediate their physical environments.

Shack Chic is an exhibition of cultural creativity in real life contexts.

Lining interior walls with branded 'wallpaper' - surplus packaging for popular South African products such as Lucky Star (pilchards), Bull Brand (corned beef), Lion matches, Sunlight soap, Colgate, Palmolive soap and Koo baked beans - is a popular décor scheme. Initially employed of necessity (functional for filling holes in the walls and covering the unsightly lack of uniformity in the building materials), they are more and more becoming a design feature in themselves. The effect of the step and repeat patterns of the paper is almost Warholian - terminally modern.

creativity

Many up-market décor shops in Cape Town and Johannesburg now offer a similar concept re-incarnated as screen-printed room partitions, lampshades, picture frames, lunch boxes and other items. The shack dwellers' inventiveness has spawned a trend that is probably the closest Sandton will ever get to Soweto in terms of aesthetic concord.

The migration from rural to urban areas has added interesting and imaginative interpretations to the creative process and transformed these mere physical dwelling places, as humble as they seem, into spiritual abodes. There is no fear of contradiction in the rural-meets-urban aesthetic that simultaneously and unapologetically juxtaposes cow horns sourced from ritual slaughter in honour of ancestors, hanging above the doorpost against Madonna-and-child icons reverently covered in protective clear plastic paper hanging on the 'living room' wall.

Photographs of loved ones are cherished in the overall scheme of décor. Usually taken by a local photographer who does the rounds daily, taking photographs of members of the community and returning on an appointed day to deliver the developed product, these cost R4 each (the average price of a loaf of bread).

commUNity

The literal meaning of 'umuntu ngumuntu nga bantu' is 'a person is a person because of other people'. In other words, you are who you are because of others. Expressed variously as 'Botho' in Sotho and Tswana, and 'Ubuntu' in the Nguni languages, this concept is about a strong sense of community where people co-exist in a mutually supportive lifestyle.

Neighbours avail themselves to mind your children while you are out looking for work. They will call in a personal favour or incur a debt on your behalf by organising a lift with someone they barely know through a 'cousin' to take your ill grandmother/spouse/child to hospital. They will take up a monetary offering in the neighbourhood or at their job in the city to help you pay your bus fare to the funeral of a distant uncle. They will even attend the funeral of someone in the area, no matter how little they knew them, as a show of support to the deceased's family.

(Someone involved in this project took an entire day off to cook and assist at the funeral of a man she had never met in her life but whom she heard came from her parents' village in the Transkei, nearly a full day's drive away. She herself was born and raised in the township and had visited Transkei only a few times in her life. Her rationale: "That's not a good way to die. I would hate to die in a place where no one knew me and no one came to my funeral.")

The larger the gathering at your passing, the greater significance your life gains. (Esther Zulu, Librarian, Mayibuye Centre). People are confident enough to migrate from the rural area of their origin on the strength of knowing someone from that area now living in the city. On arrival, they can expect to be hosted *gratis* until they find a job and place of their own. Irrespective of blood ties, significant as those are in African terms, in this peri-urban context, for purposes of maintaining social order, security, communion, financial and moral support, you 'choose' people as your family and they choose you.

In the end, this is the most prized feature of life in the informal settlement.

'umuntu ngumuntu 'nga bantu'

Ancient African maxim

line

order

colOur

go

texture

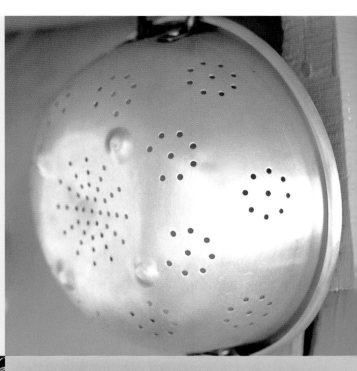

spirit

light

'temples are never built in one day. but mine, this' shack, was built in half a day'

Sandile Dikeni

Lines chart definitions, mark boundaries and establish connections, confining and releasing all at once.
Lines suggest movement. Lines suggest connections... between things, ideas and even people.
Lines arrest visual attention.

line

Shack chic is a certain style. It is spurning the conventions of geometry and creating more spontaneous configurations that lift Colgate, Kiwi, Lucky Star and Lion matches, those ubiquitous icons of South African consumerism, to recognisable and distinctive cultural symbols. A surface simplicity that belies the deeper irony of an object/user relationship in which the unattainable promises of commercial messaging clash rudely against the realities of a sector of the population that can barely afford some of the basic items that grace their humble walls.

It is, as with everything in the informal settlements, the relationship of the conscious and the unconscious that makes it truly unique.

'if there are never any vISitorS, that is not a home'

MCITWA NDABA, NO.83, SPECIAL QUARTER, LANGA

'We have a sense of communalism as opposed to individualism...
a remarkable culture of compassion.'
GEORGE BANJWA, DIRECTOR OF SENTINAL FOODS, MANDELA PARK

'Home, it's where your great people are, where you get blessings,
where the graves of your grandparents are.'
NOMA AFRICA SWELINDAWO

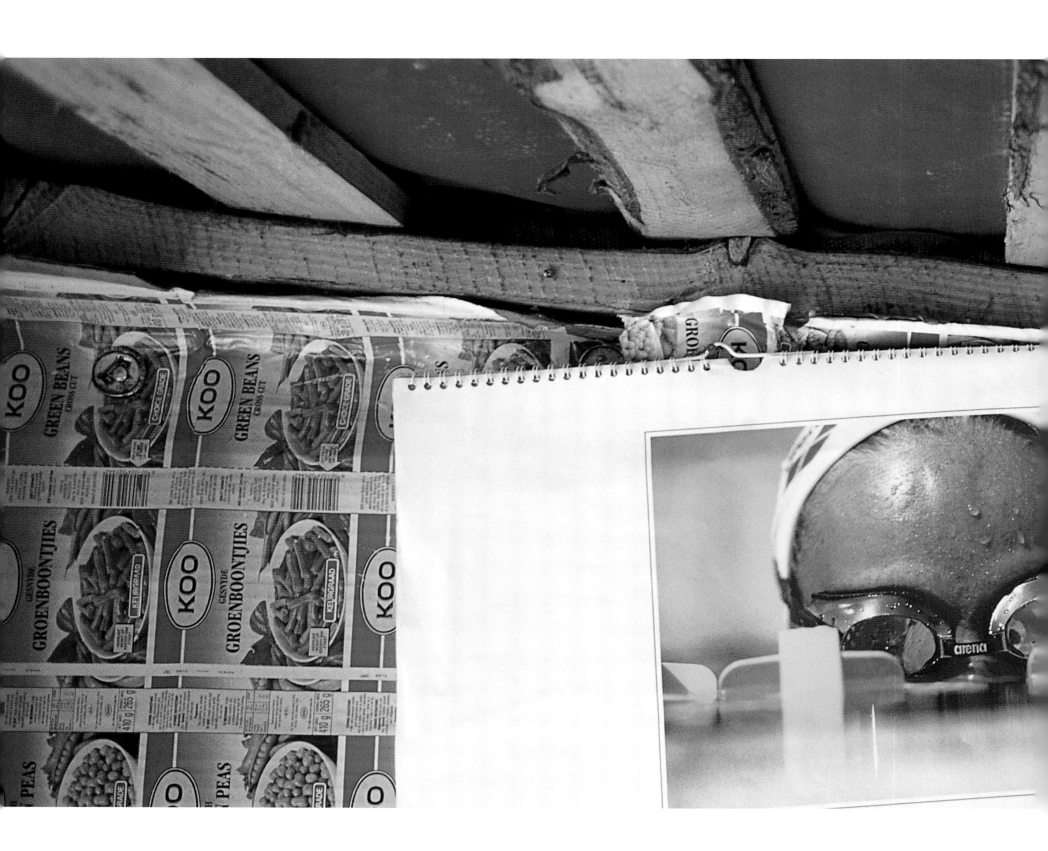

'it is
love
in the home that
builds it,
and that is what makes us
happy'

MCITWA NDABA, NO.83, SPECIAL QUARTER, LANGA

'I work as a cleaner
at De Villiers Interiors.

I learnt

deSignIng

ropes from my
grandmother, who was a
well-known designer in her

village'

LAWRENCE SIKHUNDLA · BLOCK 8, NO.166, PHILIPPI

shack prices: wooden
5m x 3m
R2400
ZinC: R3500
no glass in windows,
no door and
nO flOOr/
foundation

'there are many ways to make

muSic.

sometimes it is a

deep blue

against the wall, a bright yellow against fear,
another red to tribute imagination, hopefully
an orange to earth bad vibes
and my black voice saying

my life is

beautiful'

Sandile Dikeni

Life is a blank canvas inviting self expression. The choice and juxtaposition of colour creates vibrant energy.

colOur

Unconventional use of colour defines Shack Chic. It is unpredictable and diverse. It follows no rules. It is both accidental and deliberate. It is constrained by resource limitations but always strikingly unique.

No two shacks are identical.

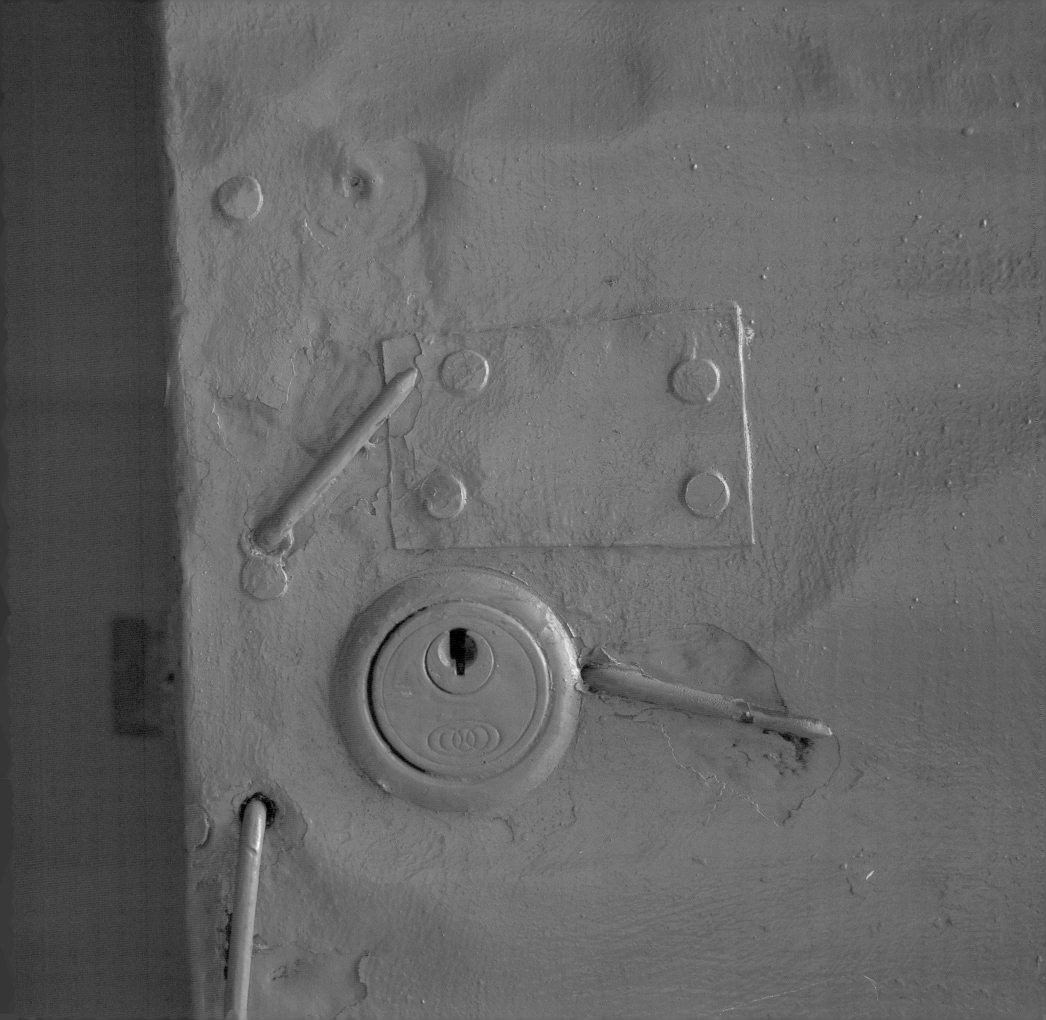

'I live pleasurably
here
for we have a
motto of treating

each other
juStly'

LAWRENCE SIKHUNDLA - BLOCK 8, NO.166, PHILIPPI

'I
love

Bob Marley most when he sings *One Love* and
Jahman's song entitled *Two Sides of Love*,
because I believe it's nothing but love that will

set us free

from hate and jealousy'

LAWRENCE SIKHUNDLA · BLOCK 8, NO.166, PHILIPPI

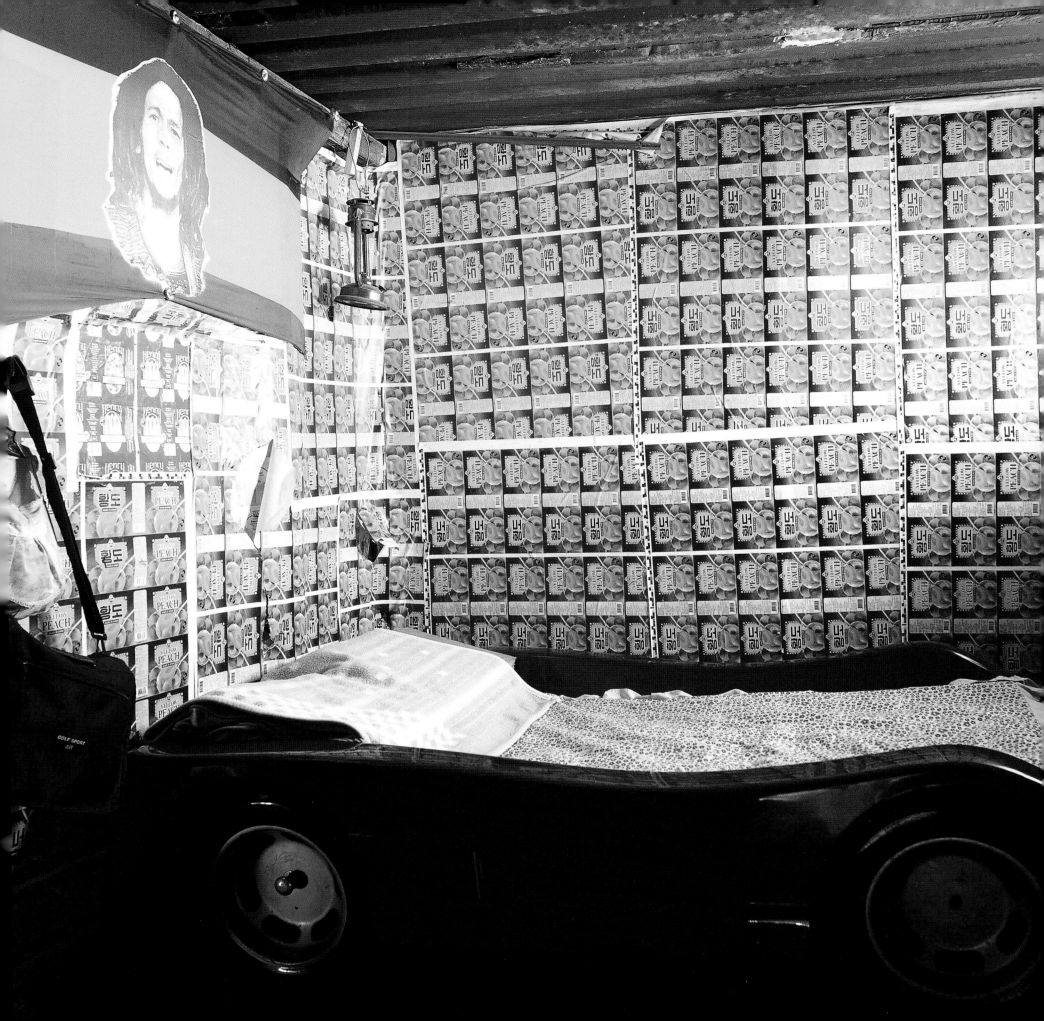

'I like a blue colour, for it brightens my home and gives my flowers an ideal background to shine and blossom.'

ELLIOT XOLANI MRHWETYANA, BROWN'S FARM, PHILIPPI

'I like bright colour. It makes me feel alive.'

NOZOLILE NAGMLANA, ROAD 21, VIETNAM, PHILIPPI

'on that
chair
there, we conceived
Sipho the gift.
that was before the bed
and a job
from Airflex Recliners (Pty) Ltd'

Sandile Dikeni

Order is the contrast of the chaos outside with the functional order of the interior. It is ten people living a collective reality in one room yet maintaining personal identities.

Order is the ability to exist, contentedly, in a space where physical confines constantly threaten to infringe on mental and spiritual liberty.

It is the process of making a space for yourself in the midst of so many people and identifying with the visible and invisible structures of the community - the how, where and when. Being accepted, choosing a site, building on it and settling in.

Order is being separate but connected.

order

'Home is where I was born, it's where my umbilical cord is.'

PHEKO MONATSI, 3571 HEMPE STR

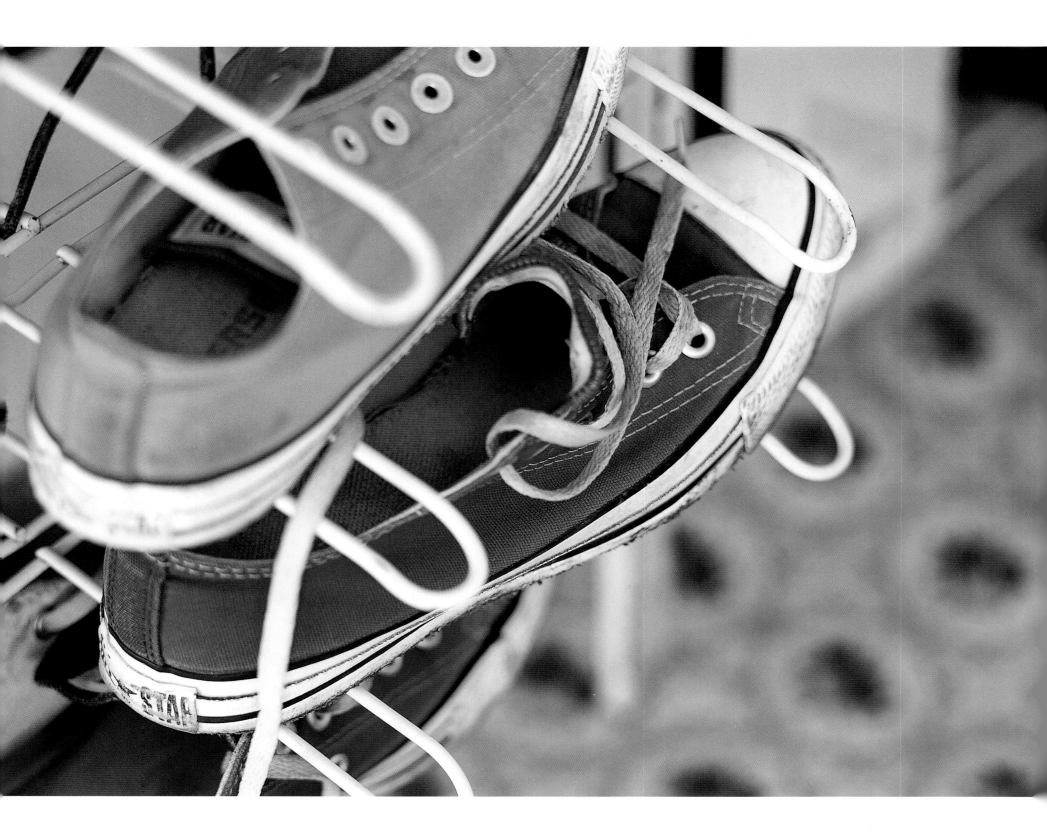

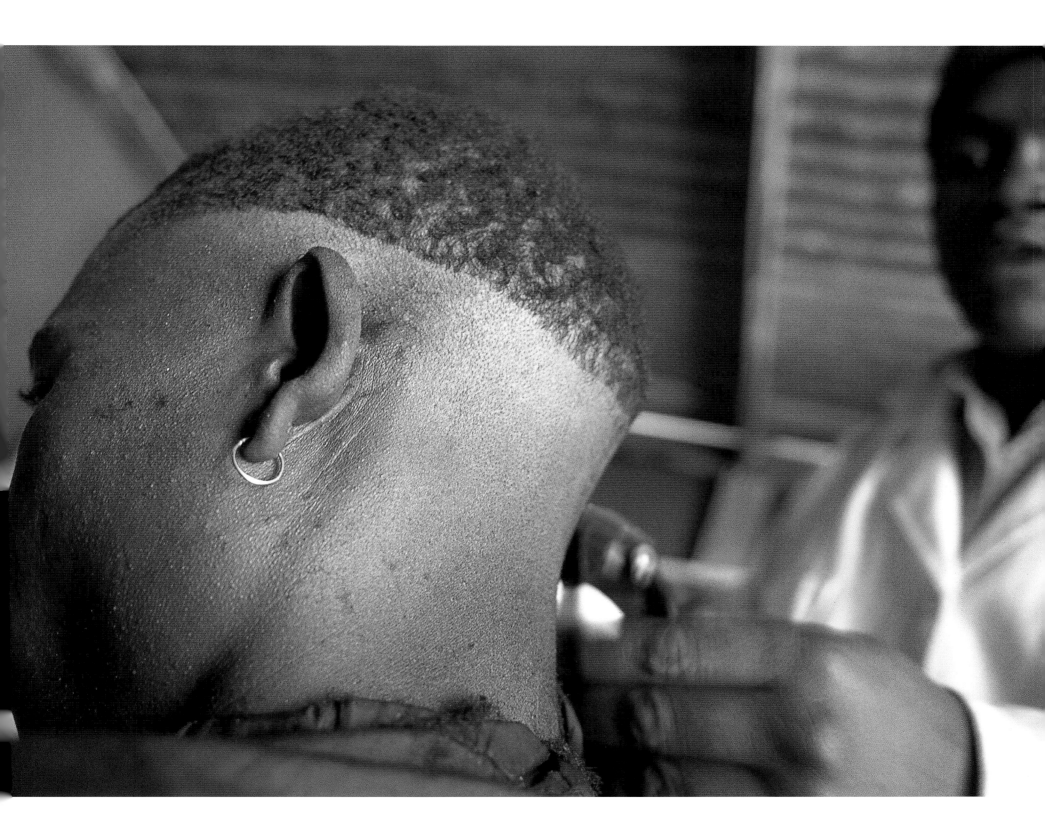

'my

artistIC

personality is reflected most in my home.

you can see

piCtures

on the wall, a collage that I am busy with
and my in-house workshop says a lot about my
personality and my

inclination if not

my destiny in life'

THEMBA MAJEBE, A31, BROWN'S FARM, PHILIPPI

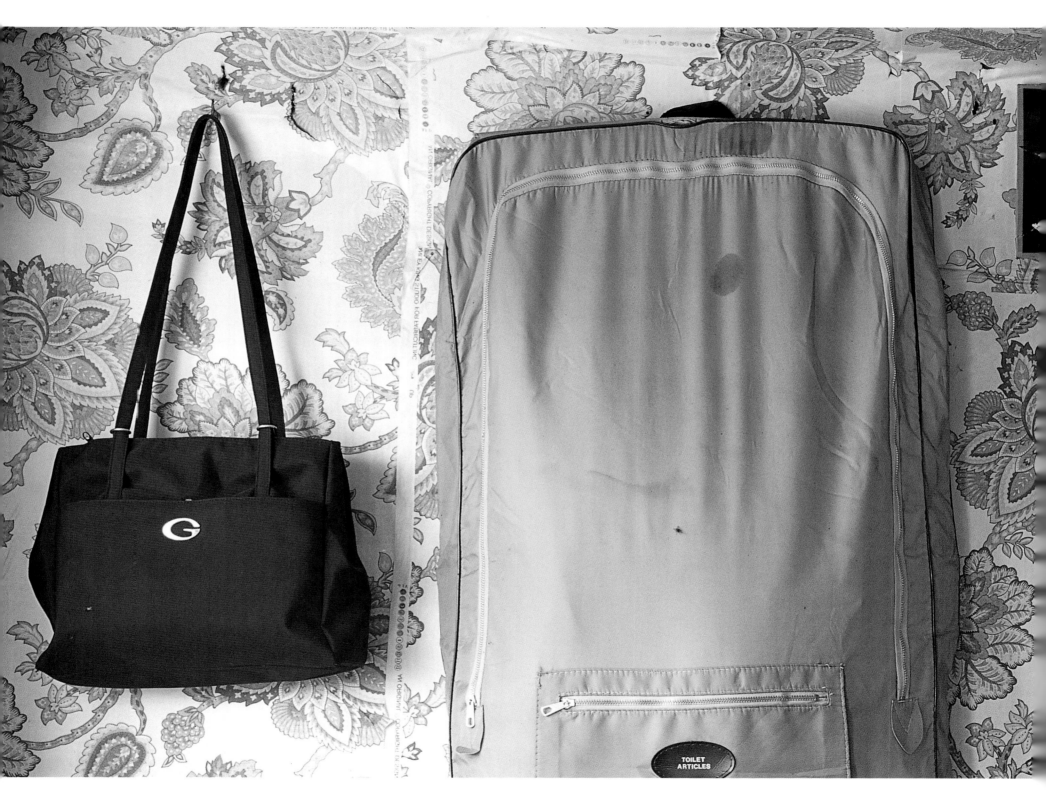

'There are community leaders in my area who are responsible for everything, like theft and running water, and to look after our area.'

NTOMBENKOSI MRADU, BROWN'S FARM, PHILIPPI

'flowers

give my home

life, colour and a

natural

beauty'

ELLIOT XOLANI MRHWETYANA, BROWN'S FARM, PHILIPPI

'There is no money that can buy that picture, it symbolises my respect and my humble honour to mother nature.'

ELLIOT XOLANI MRHWETYANA, BROWN'S FARM, PHILIPPI

' as a Xhosa woman,
that three-legged pot
means the most to me.
we cook on pots such as these
when preparing a meal for the
rites of passage
ritual,
or traditional
ceremonies'

NOZOLILE NGAMLANA, ROAD 21, VIETNAM, PHILIPPI

'je**S**us
was not born here
but sometimes he comes in
through the little
holes
in the walls and
sits on that chair'

Sandile Dikeni

spirit

A home reflects something of the owner's cultural background and personality ... or at least, it should.

So what is it about a house that makes it a home? Which are the important elements and which not? The roof? The doors? The floors? Or the more intangible things ... communion, comfort, warmth and refuge?

There is no doubt that there is a direct relationship between physical comfort and psychological ease. It therefore follows that it is impossible to be mentally at ease in materially constrained circumstances. Or does it?

Shack Chic is about people being proud, satisfied and even happy despite obvious financial, educational, social and political limitations. It is the readiness to be generous not only with one's means but with one's very self, to be charitable even when one has nothing.

It is the melding together of traditional ways and beliefs with new found urban survival tactics.

'a
hOme
without a
mOther
is not a home'

THEMBA MAJEBE, A31, BROWN'S FARM, PHILIPPI

'I think it is my duty that if I succeed I don't succeed alone.'

GEORGE BANJWA, DIRECTOR OF SENTINAL FOODS, MANDELA PARK

'A home means so much and everything to me - it's where my spirit resides, it's where I communicate with my ancestors in their visits at night in my dreams.'

LAWRENCE SIKHUNDLA · BLOCK 8, No.166, PHILIPPI

'I hate **private** life ... I grew up at a **home** where everyone at every time was **welcomed'**

GEORGE BANJWA, DIRECTOR OF SENTINAL FOODS, MANDELA PARK

'We live as if we were born by the same parents. They will pick me up when I am down, they will clothe me when I am naked and they will definitely feed me when I am hungry.'
THEMBA MAJEBE, A31, BROWN'S FARM, PHILIPPI

'If there is an overproduction of fish I don't wait for it to get rotten. I bring it here and
give it to people while it's still fresh, for free.'

GEORGE BANJWA, DIRECTOR OF SENTINAL FOODS, MANDELA PARK

'there is something
sensual
about the
rattle
of rain
on a
corrugated roof'

Sandile Dikeni

'Texture: the character, appearance or consistency of a surface or a textile fabric as determined by the arrangement and thickness of its threads.'

Based on the above dictionary definition, Shack Chic is about texture in huge amounts. The surfaces are a multi-media patchwork of wood grain, plastic, cardboard, sand, zinc, vinyl, concrete, brick, cotton, satin, sisal, paper, mud, fine dust, chicken feathers, crocheted bedspreads, wool, curly hair ...

texture

In this eclectic mix of textures, Shack Chic expressively mirrors the reality of life - shiny and dull in patches, hard and soft in places, tough and fragile in turn.

The discarded rudiments of other people's pasts are reincarnated into vibrant and living elements of the present. In a society where practically everything is obtained second or third hand, found objects are shaken free of their previous associations to take on a whole new and permanent part in the life of the home.

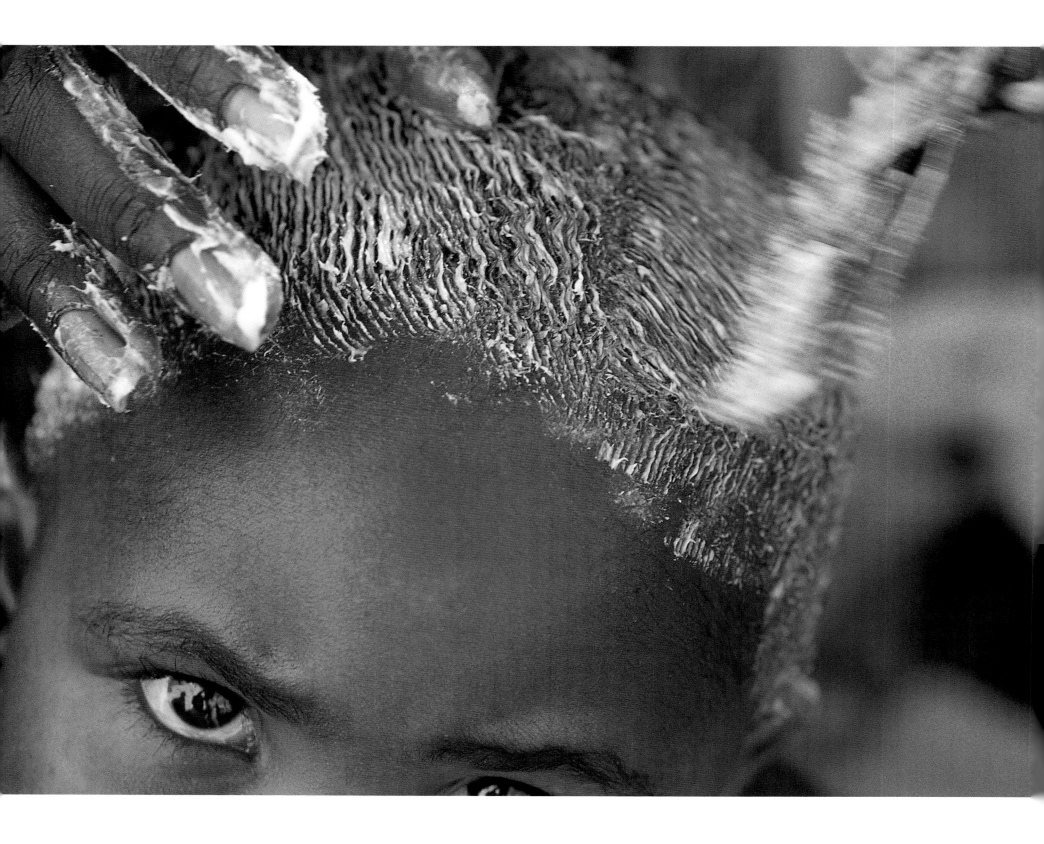

'I would cook rice, meat, pumpkin, beans and soup for guests.'

NONDAZA NDAEAMBI, 36122, HEMPE STR., MAKHAZA

'When I am home I walk barefoot in the kraal, telling my ancestors I am back.'

NOMA AFRIKA, SOLIDANE MAKHAZA, MBEKO STR., 36022

'I believe that if you are

clean,

chances are

your

heart

is also clean'

LAWRENCE SIKHUNDLA · BLOCK 8, NO.166, PHILIPPI

'We are five. The three children are not mine, they were left by their mother who passed away.'
NOMA AFRIKA, SOLIDANE MAKHAZA, 36022, MBEKO STR.

'after the rain,
earth, as whiff, comes
knocking on my fragile door.
earth as
fragrance
embracing the musk
and unmasking the undressed breath of another night
of tender love making
under the naughty stars peeping
through the
transparency
of a revealing
plastic roof'

Sandile Dikeni

light

Sunlight, candlelight, lamplight, torchlight, electric light ... Whatever form it comes in, light is coveted by the human species for more than the mere purpose of dispelling darkness.

It is the one element that is able to create mood and lend magic even to the most humble space. It creates a natural flow between interior and exterior and has a supernatural energy that promotes a sense of spaciousness even in the most cramped dwelling.

Shack Chic is the delightful lustre of light as it falls on the reflective surfaces of highly polished furniture, zinc wash buckets and a thousand foil wrappers. It is the ambience, dream-like in quality, that illuminates objects, elevating them from their mundane status to an almost fantastical surreal transparency.

'I do the paintings by using coloured papers.'
NTOMBENKOSI MRADU, 51, BROWN'S FARM, PHILIPPI

'I would love my children to see the wOrld through their own black spectacles'

GEORGE BANJWA, DIRECTOR OF SENTINAL FOODS, MANDELA PARK

'I miss the stars and that darkness and also to see those women with clay on their faces.'
NTOMBENKOSI MRADU, 51, BROWN'S FARM, PHILIPPI

'the tentacles of despair are
challenged by the soft touches
of eternal determination.
many times between void and void
it is only us
testifying to creative
eSSence
aS hope'

Sandile Dikeni

'Home is both my material and spiritual treasure. It's where I prepare and end my day's journey.'
LAWRENCE SIKHUNDLA · BLOCK 8, NO.166, PHILIPPI

Jackson Baduza, Brown's Farm, Philippi

George Banjwa, Mandela Park, Hout Bay

Themba Baye, Philippi

Mr and Mrs Justice Baza, Zone 18, Langa

Patience Dona, Mon Wood, Philippi

Mfhunzi Duba, Brown's Farm, Philippi

Sipho Dumalisile, Irene Street, Somerset West

Amanda Dyibane

Wilfred Feni, Zone 2, Langa

Sihle Galeni, Khayelitsha

V. George, Saywithi Street, Philippi

Sindiswe Goduka, Village 4, Philippi

Witness Hlaku, Old Flats, Langa

Melikhaya Jack, New Flats, Langa

William Jibani, Brown's Farm, Philippi

Aubrey Jumba, Langa

Indipile Kalipha

Mandis Khamnqa, Zone 1, Langa

Zanemulila Ngetsheni, Philippi

Sidwell Monatsi Lebetsa, Khayelitsha

Nyalleng Lerole

Bahle Luvalo, Khayelitsha

Nosiseko Mace, Philippi

Cynthia Mahijana, New Flats, Langa

Nolonwabo Magazi, New Flats, Langa

Nosango Magazi

Xolile Magazi, Brown's Farm, Philippi

Volat Makeleni, Vietnam, Philippi

Mlunaisi Makhawula, Philippi

Themba Majebe, Brown Wood, Philippi

Gloria Malzz, New Flats, Langa

Elliot Magoswana, Khayelitsha

Nokanyiso Magoswana, Khayelitsha

Daniel Marion Jr, New Crossroads, Nyanga

Nozwelethu Matshisi, New Flats, Langa

Isaac Mbane, Gugulethu

Nomlandelo Mbombi, Langa

Simon Memene, Brown's Farm, Philippi

Bonisile Mfundisi, Village 3, Philippi

Jackson Mhlabeni, Gugulethu

Noxolisile Mgolombane

Sthembele Minana, Brown Wood, Philippi

Sipho Mpinga, Zone 1, Langa

Agnes Mradu, Brown's Farm, Philippi

Nontilili Msaro, Brown's Farm, Philippi

Wakke Mtembu, Mtsha Street, Lusaka,

Patricia Mthothwa, New Flats, Langa

Miliswa Mtsocongo, New Flats, Langa

Miriam Nadikida, Brown's Farm, Philippi

Minki Nake, New Flats, Langa

Victoria Nasiphi, Brown's Farm, Philippi

Nosicelo Ndabambi, Hempe Street, Khayelitsha

Iris Ndebu, Brown's Farm, Philippi

Nopasika Ndesana, New Flats, Langa

Linda Ndgala, Old Flats, Langa

Nozlile Ngamlana, Vietnam, Philippi

Nothemba Ngolo, Langa

Malibongwe Ngotyana, Gugulethu

Busisiwe Ngxonono, Mon Wood, Philippi

Benedicta Njokweni

Zukisa Nkonde, New Flats, Langa

Nie Nobokwana, Philippi

Richard Nozigawaba, Brown's Farm, Philippi

Sidney Nzima, P.S.G. Hostel, Langa

Ntombonina Seya, Philippi

Thandiswe Sigam, New Flats, Langa

Zukile Sihu, Khayelitsha

Bukeka Sitsha, Zone 2, Langa

Herbert Sityashe, Gugulethu

Lawrence Skundla, Philippi

Mavis Sokuyeka, Brown's Farm, Philippi

Princess Somdaka, Brown Wood, Philippi

St Johns Apostolic Church, Langa

Norma Africa Swelindawo, Khayelitsha

Ntombovuyo Tatase, K.T.C., Nyanga

Nceba Tyeni, One Heart, Philippi

Mrs B. van der Merwe, Vietnam, Franschhoek

Nomzi Wanteka, New Flats, Langa

Mzukisi Zele, Brown's Farm, Phillipi,

Naphtali Zindlovu, K.T.C., Nyanga

Nolenzola Zuntsi, Zone 21, Langa

thanks

'these walls,
thin as membranes,
keep nothing
outSide.
they are here
to keep our beauty inside,
away from that
solitude
out there'

Sandile Dikeni

CRAIG FRASER (PHOTOGRAPHER)

Craig Fraser studied journalism and Mass Media Studies at Rhodes University.

A freelance photographer, specialising in interiors, he has travelled internationally photographing homes and commercial installations. His work has been published in several South African magazines, most notably *Elle, Habitat* and *House and Leisure* as well as internationally in *Elle,* and in books published by Carlton and Quadrille. His most recent book is titled *Stylish Living in South Africa.*

LIBEY DOYLE (GRAPHIC DESIGNER)

Libby Doyle studied at Michaelis School of Art and Architecture at the University of Cape Town. She then went on to study Basic Design in Black and White and Print Techniques in Boston, Massachusetts.

After spending four years working at various agencies in Cape Town, she started Hero Design and Advertising, which she sold five years later, going on to work at Wechsler & Partners in New York for two years.

Doyle Design, an agency based in Cape Town specialising in product design, has been running since 1997.

TAWENI GONDWE (WRITER)

Taweni holds a BA in Linguistics and Literature and a Post-graduate Diploma in Copywriting. In her writing career she has been the recipient of several international awards.

She has contributed to various magazines including *Vodaworld* and *Cosmopolitan* and has written and edited a book on behalf of FIFA honouring Nelson Mandela.

Formerly editor of *Design Indaba Magazine,* a special interest magazine targeting the advertising and design industries, she is currently editor of *O, The Oprah Magazine* in South Africa.

SANDILE DIKENI (POET)

Sandile Dikeni, a poet and columnist, is the author of two collections of poetry, *Guava Juice* (Mayibuye Books 1992) and *Telegraph to the Sky* (University of Natal Press 2000). His work has also been anthologised in many journals and collaborations including Staffrider (SA), New Observations (New York), Wasafiri (London), Khayelitsha: 14-2-95, a collaboration with Alesandro Esteri (Italy). He has been translated into French, Hebrew and Italian.

His collection of columns and articles, *Soul Fire* (University of Natal Press 2000), has just been released. He currently lives in Pretoria.

ABLE MPUTING (JOURNALIST)

Before enrolling at UCT he studied creative writing. In 1992 he obtained a Diploma in Jazz Theory and obtained a third grade in classical theory with distinction. After finishing his music diploma, he became a co-founder of The Jam band and recorded a song on a CD compilation with the New World Music company.

During the course of his degree at UCT he also studied film, English and literature, and joined the Afro African Film Resource Organisation. In 1998, he accepted a post as an Assistant Cultural Officer at the Centre for African Studies at UCT.

He now works as a freelance writer and contributes to publications such as *The Cape Times, Tribute Magazine, Sunday World, Big Issue* and *Cape Argus*.

MLUNGISI GEGANA (OUR GUIDE AND TRANSLATOR)

Mlungisi grew up in a farming town in the Eastern Cape. He started playing music when he was 12 years old using a three string guitar which he had made from nylon and a five litre tin.

In 1986 Mlungisi went to Cape Town to further his musical career. He met bassist, Godfrey Ntsila, and took the bass up as his preferred instrument. Self-taught, he played for various local bands.

Subsequently, Mlungisi studied a few years of music at MAPP School of Music at the University of Cape Town but was forced to give up due to lack of funds. He is now a freelance bass player, living in Johannesburg.